Million Dollar Mistakes in New Home Marketing
..Expert Advice On How To Do It Right!

Alan Daniel with Robert Cowes

MILLION DOLLAR

MISTAKES

IN NEW HOME

MARKETING

..Expert Advice On How To Do It Right!

By Alan Daniel with Robert Cowes
Cofounders of
SmartTouch®

To our families and dedicated staff,

we are so thankful.

FORWARD

Alan and I have known each other since 2010, when I met him at a Seminar at the International Builders Show in Orlando, FL. I immediately recognized that his software SmartTouch was unlike anything we had on the market in Toronto, Canada and invited him to explore our market, which is one of the most dynamic in North America. He has since seen his client list grow and grow in our market as others found success using his methods.

Our firm has participated in the marketing of over 2,000 communities across North America. One of our mantras to builders is "You are not in the business of *building* homes. You are in the business of *selling* homes. The building is only the reward you get after you sell! Builders often put sales and marketing last on their list, when it really should be first.

I have read Alan's book *Million Dollar Mistakes in New Home Marketing* cover to cover. It contains an immense amount of relevant data, thoughts and practical knowledge that are the sum of his experience and expertise gained over many years. The book provides a valuable window into the world of online lead generation and technology including practical ideas that can be easily implemented for their marketing and sales.

I recommend this book to all hoping to succeed in the world of real estate marketing.

McOUAT | PARTNERSHIP

Lianne McOuat

TABLE OF CONTENTS

Introduction

By Alan Daniel & Robert Cowes

Marketing absurdities have blinded new home builders and developers into thinking the most successful way to sell property is through real estate agents and traditional efforts. Sales and marketing efforts of the past are simply that, in the past. To the point - why aren't you selling $100,000,000 worth of real estate? Why aren't you selling ALL of your available inventory as fast as projected? Why are you sitting on unsold new homes, condos or beautiful lots longer than you projected? Or simply, why is your marketing budget not working for you?

Well, of course you don't control the market, but you may be in a rut and need to try something new. Are you doing the same thing you have always done and expecting different results? It is the purest definition of insanity.

As an example, builders and developers have traditionally relied heavily upon real estate agents to sell new homes and condos, thus giving away 2 to 4 percent profit on every sale through commissions. Unfortunately, for most home builders and developers, that's as much as $400,000 of lost profit on every $10,000,000 of revenue.

The message of this simple book isn't to stop using Realtors, but it is to start using the technology that is easily at your disposal. We like to say," Technology won't replace Realtors, but it will replace your dependency on Realtors as a primary strategy to be successful at new home marketing and sales.

Google is not the neighborhood café. It's not a doorknob, a postcard nor a welcome mat. As a builder, you must consistently reach out locally through Realtors and maintain those relationships. But if you are using Realtors to sell more than 30% of your homes, you aren't using all the tools in your toolbox. Unlike Realtor programs, a strategic online marketing campaign with an appropriate Call to Action ("CTA") which reaches hundreds of thousands of buyers will instantly create direct buyers and empower you with new tools available to educate, incubate, and cultivate relationships directly. Converting online inquiries or leads into direct sales will radically reduce your cost of sales and increase your bottom line.

If I have your attention, read on. The interactive advertising firm my co-founder, Robert Cowes, and I started years ago has spent millions of builder's advertising dollars to learn these lessons. We have spent millions on our technology solution (SmartTouch®) to track success and failures for builders and developers. If I've lost your attention, or if you aren't interested in trying something new or hearing some crazy stories about business, building companies, and the high stakes of the internet, then feel free to give this book to someone you think might enjoy it.

The goal of this short book is to pass on a few hard-learned lessons, arm you with new methods that accelerate sales, and help you make a significant change in your marketing and sales approach. Even if you don't drastically change your ways, you could be entertained by what we, our team, our partners, and our clients have learned along the way, so I do hope you will read on.

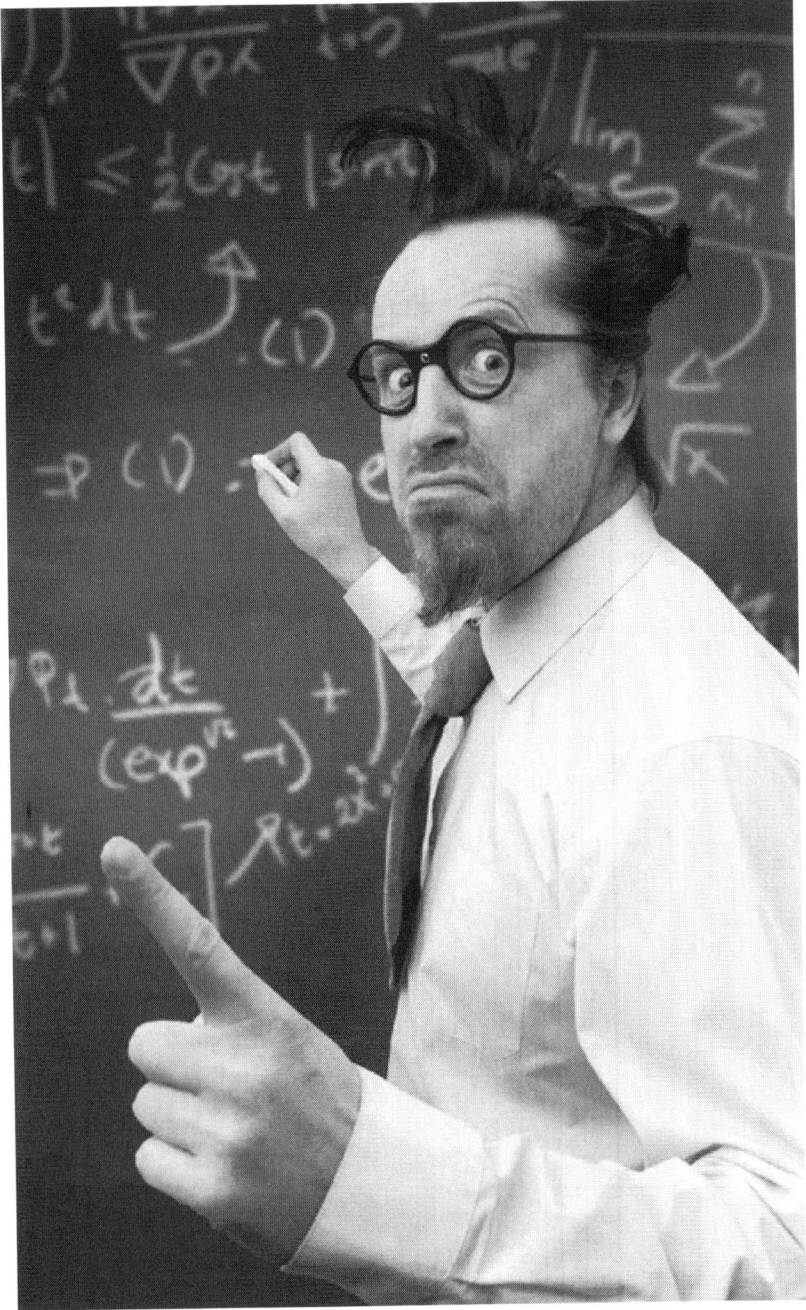

Simple Math

By Alan Daniel

Recently I was included in a panel at the International Builder's Show (IBS) speaking on the 50 top marketing strategies for new home builders and developers. Over the past 10 years, my last 3 companies have created 50 billion in real estate sales online (www.MetroSceneTV.com, www.LandsofAmerica.com, & www.SmartTouchInteractive.com). The panel also included David Miles, who has won 92 creative design awards for his creative work, and Jennifer Hurst, who has sold over 3 billion dollars in real estate in multi-builder communities and was named the IBS Marketing Professional of the Year. Lianne McOuat, who runs a 2nd generation agency in Toronto whose clients have sold over 20 billion dollars in real estate was also on the panel.

During the panel discussion, we took 25 successfully proven online marketing tactics from the panel and 25 tactics from the crowd. Immediately after hearing the panel's 25 online and digital tactics, the attendees began to share their best practices with marketing to Realtors. After the 4th Realtor marketing story, I had enough. I literally stopped the woman dead in the middle of her sentence. I needed to stop this thinking, or the discussion would have continued in the direction of how to expand Realtor programs. Like most of the group, this poor woman didn't recognize that our top 25 best interactive marketing tactics are changing the reliance on Realtors AND these tactics are saving builders and developers millions.

If your marketing team can't generate direct buyers and your sales team can't sell to buyers without Realtors, fire them. When I said to the audience, "If you can't reduce your cost of acquisition from 4 percent (Realtor commission) to 1.5 percent (marketing budget), then why have a website at all, and why 'market' at all? Why attend an interactive session to learn online lead generation and talk about Realtor marketing programs?" I think they finally began to get it. But rest assured, mouths were agape.

Give the online strategies and tactics in this book a marketing budget of 2.5 percent to 4 percent of your new home sales volume, and you will sell houses faster. You could sell more property without realtor representation and you will see more profitability because of it. Crazy, you say? Consider this: your cost of sales can climb as high as 6 percent in tough markets. That cost of acquisition is ridiculous! It's nonsense! Could reducing the amount you're paying in external commissions be the solution? Not completely. But it is a critical part of the equation.

This mentality is not NEW math. I am not trying to change mathematical equations. I am trying to help builders and developers make sense of the new interactive world we live in and capitalize on new online buyer behavior. Not many in the IBS audience had considered the direct interactive approach when they entered our session. After overcoming their initial resistance, it was clear the crowd liked the thought of reducing high commissions and saving money. People began to understand these new economic metrics. The benefit of online marketing directly to consumer is not a difficult concept to grasp. It is, however, a completely opposite mindset from the traditional paradigm of the new home builder selling 80 percent of his properties through agents.

Times have changed and buyers are researching purchases online before they ever talk to a live person. From social media to retargeting for Google Ads, there are hundreds of online options and channels for builders to reach new buyers.

As an internet marketer & technologist, my job is to find your customers and buyers online, directly, without charging you a percentage of your revenue in commission. The results could reduce overall acquisition cost by simply having a process to work more of the leads directly. As a builder or developer, you want to transfer the Realtor fee to a marketing investment and builder profit. From my perspective, it is simple math. Realtor programs + online marketing strategies = good investment and accelerated sales. One without the other is only half the equation.

All Sizzle, No Steak

By Alan Daniel

The launch of *"MetrosceneTV: The Hottest Properties in Chicago"* was a red carpet event at Park West Theatre in Chicago for a who's who group in the Chicago real estate industry: the largest developers in the country with celebrity *starchitects* (such as David Brininstool and Helmut Jahn). The buzz in the community was that condos featured in this hot new television series would sell themselves, and buyers would be lining up at the door to purchase pre-phase condos in the most desirable parts of the city. It created the necessary momentum every builder wants for a project. The television show was effective on the front-end launch, but not effective as the sole strategy for selling the building. This is a story about poor assumptions and lessons learned.

"MetroScene", the 26-week series, featured over twenty separate developments and drove viewers to the website MetrosceneTV.com. In general, builders spent $65,000 to $120,000 to generate 24 specific leads at a cost of about $2,500 per specific lead. The hard costs, media costs, and time investment became a losing proposition. The average cost per lead for a builder was not sustainable, killing any chance we had as a production company to maintain a business model and an ongoing business concern. It was sexy, but not sustainable.

But we didn't know it at the time. We thought we had this all figured out.

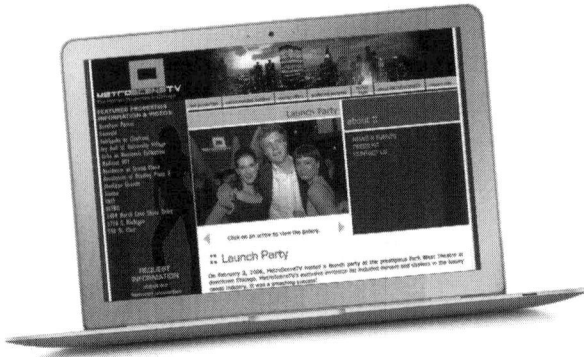

At the time, the real estate market was booming. We had an exceptionally creative team and produced a sophisticated, sexy and exclusive television experience for high-end condo buyers. In developing MetrosceneTV, which aired on Fox in Chicago, I learned that despite the buzz, without results the business model was not sustainable. Buzz is great for our creative liberty and our egos, but it doesn't sell condos.

We had high production costs, high media costs and a high fashion lifestyle magazine host, Roni Proter. Roni featured and interviewed the best designers, builders and developers, chefs and shops in the most exclusive Chicago neighborhoods. It was geared to and for an exclusive life of luxury. We featured the "lifestyle" outside of price and floor plans. We also featured exclusive attributes and amenities, local information, and all the specific appeal related to the neighborhood and niche markets. But what we failed to do was generate specific and qualified leads for each individual condo development. We generated general leads for condo buyers in the Chicago area, but not for each specific project.

In the end, the TV experience was an awesome personal experience for everyone involved, but it was not a good business model for immediate, specific, lead generation. Builders and developers might look back and say they wish they had invested their marketing dollars differently because MetrosceneTV wasn't able to generate specific leads needed to move units in the time required.

If you have a large marketing budget that includes television that's okay. At the end of the day, building a brand isn't a lost cause. Television may be okay as part of the mix, but it is no substitute for a true lead generation campaign.

This boils down to one point: the cost of television production and TV eyeballs far exceeds content creation costs for digital advertising and online traffic. Without a standard framework for making decisions on investing advertising dollars, how in the world can anyone make the right choices? To make online advertising work (or any advertising option for that matter) you must understand a few new metrics: "cost per lead" and "cost per tour/showing."

A concept that catches most builders off guard is that technology allows us to drive down the cost per lead and cost per sale while at the same time improving our ability to track everything. If you're using outdated strategies and methods that don't reflect today's environment, you're relying on gut instinct and emotion. Math isn't emotional.

Builders and developers must use analytics to ensure a measurable return on investment. Television will never be able to offer such analytics. Developers loved the television

experience, but the end result was not profitable. As some

would say, it was "All Sizzle, No Steak."

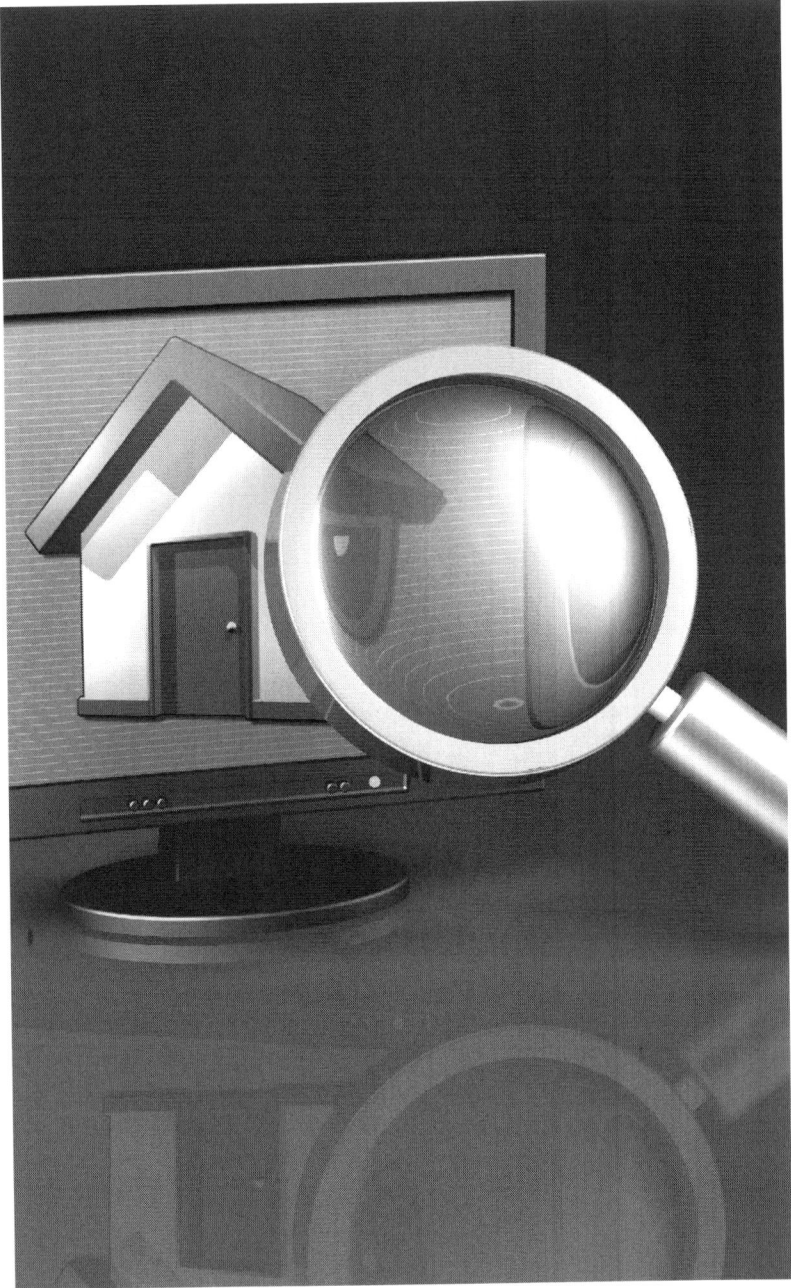

Why Real Estate Portals Work

By Alan Daniel

For brokers and agents who advertise, or home builders and developers who measure return on marketing investment, we have a question for you. How would you respond if offered the opportunity to pay $10 for a specific buyer (lead) interested in a specific property? Common sense says at the very least you'd at the very least give it a try. Right?

These focused, affordable, online buyer leads are what put television advertising for real estate out of business, in my opinion. I learned this first hand at Lands of America, a 3rd party listing aggregator with 40 billion dollars' worth of property listings. Basically, Lands of America is an online listing aggregator of rural land for sale.

The story that follows is why third-party listing portals work (e.g. Zillow, Trulia, New Home Source). There is an urban legend that Southwest Airlines Founder Herb Kelleher sat at a bar and drew out his concept for a commuter airline on a bar napkin. Well, one morning at 7:30, over coffee and tacos at a Wimberley, Texas hole-in-the-wall, I decided to join an old friend with his idea of Internet land MLS after he basically sketched it on his napkin.

What happened over the next three years is a story of tremendous growth, acceleration and great success. Lands of America was a model that leveraged technology, not traditional high-touch sales methods. Low personal touch and high technology – the opposite of traditional real estate sales tactics - were the key. We had 8,000 rural Realtors listing 102,000 properties worth 40 billion dollars. In 3 years, before the company sold to LoopNet (which later sold to Co Star), LandsofAmerica.com grew the average unique visitors per month from 2,000 to 200,000. When you have 200,000 property buyers per month it's a win, win, win! It was a win for Lands of America, it was a win for the seller and it was a win for the buyers. It was a tremendous success in real estate marketing. US Land and Ranches, Bluegreen Communities, Southerland Properties, hundreds of low-density developers, and 8,000 Realtors were all able to experience an amazing return on investment.

We were generating 25,000 leads per month, which worked out to 3 unique leads per month for the marginal cost of $30 per month for the 8,000 sellers we worked with. For most land sellers, discovering LandsofAmerica.com was like discovering gold. From a marketing perspective, comparing the high cost of leads from MetrosceneTV to what we could accomplish at LandsofAmerica.com made me quickly realize why MetrosceneTV was not sustainable.

Further, when our builder, broker and developer clients compared the marginal numbers from their own web traffic to the staggering statistics for their page views on a real estate listing portal (aggregator) it was a no-brainer.

To be more specific, LandsofAmerica.com won the organic search game on Google. For example, searching the name of any top land broker, rather than their personal website, their listing page on LandsofAmerica.com would rank #1 on page 1. We generated thousands of first page search results for brokers and developers, while the developers or brokers own website was not visible until page 6. In addition, LoA won thousands of generic keywords for rural real estate in organic search for Google, Bing and Yahoo. It's called the "long tail" and it represents the millions of combinations people use to search the Internet for property for sale. Just imagine the endless combinations. We won them all:

> Land for Sale Texas
>
> Texas Ranch for Sale
>
> Texas Rural Properties

Rural properties for sale in Texas

Available Land in Texas

Texas Rural Land

Acreage Lots for Sale

Country Homes

Like LandsofAmerica.com, there are a few major players doing a great job of connecting property sellers with buyers. It's crucial for all real estate specialists to find the real estate portals that help you find your target buyers. Not only do property portals work, they can literally make or break a seller or project and your annual income. We've seen it hundreds of times at SmartTouch®.

Real Estate Sales and Dating

By Robert Cowes

Selling a new home is akin to dating. How many sales people try to close a deal on the first phone call or first tour? Are you going to get to the altar on the first date? It is highly unlikely.

The *old school* methodology used by some sales people to close on the first connection is changing. Some great sales agents can schedule a tour on the first call, but most cannot. A hard, quick close or conversion is the equivalent of proposing on your first date. The real method that works today is getting to know your buyer by asking questions, learning about his or her interests and establishing a mutually beneficial relationship.

Great builders, developers and sales teams understand that buyers have considerations outside of price and floor plan and it is absolutely critical to engage the buyer in that subjective piece of the conversation. You need to understand the local information, attributes and amenities, and specific demographic information that appeals to a buyer. A buyer may go "dark" or mysteriously disappear if your marketing and sales team are not helpful in all facets of the buyer's decision process. To attract an Internet buyer, a builder has to be attractive. That requires your marketing and sales team to have specific, helpful information that goes much deeper than just price and floor plan. Your team must also have knowledge of each individual buyer. Not only must your team's communication reflect knowledge of your community, products and your specific floor plans, but more importantly a great sales person will understand the buyer's reaction to all these variables. Building a quality relationship requires you to know your buyer. That means being ultra-responsive, it means being patient and communicating on their time, and being available on nights or weekends and early mornings (outside your shift or model home hours of operation).

Just as offline sales conversations build relationships, so can marketing campaigns, if they are built on specific interests. In Texas, our interactive agency concluded that all television advertising, and print as well for that matter, for real estate sales is the equivalent of a shotgun approach (please pardon the analogy, but I am from Texas). A shotgun sprays and covers a broad area, generating awareness, but misses the specific buyer with immediate needs. Where television is a shotgun, Google Adwords (SEM) and search engine optimization (SEO) or any inbound online marketing, is your rifle, a laser-targeted approach to connecting your home for sale with buyers at the exact point of their particular interest. TV, radio, and print are one-to-many communications, whereas interactive advertising is one to one.

Builders and developers can now engage with a buyer at their precise interest and pain points. This is a new paradigm that some builders and developers, on occasion, have trouble embracing. Interactive lead generation is meeting a buyer at their exact point of need and interest and beginning a "digital conversation".

In slow and difficult markets, analytics from our SmartTouch® CRM report that 290 days and 52 touch points are required to manage a prospective home buyer from early research to actual transaction. It is one of the biggest decisions of a buyer's life, and it requires time. As mentioned earlier, some great sales people are trained to create value and can close on the first tour. As a sophisticated builder, your marketing and sales team have to think through content strategies that connect with home buyers early and keep the conversation and relationship alive from the first inquiry to 6th tour. Knowing it takes up to 290 days and 52 touch points to create a sale, shouldn't we be thinking about the buyer and what information they'll need over the decision-making time period?

How many marketing departments have developed strategies to continue to engage the buyer? In our experience, very few new home builders and developers understand it. Imagine a new home buyer going to New Home Source, Trulia, or Zillow to seek information on an area or property. They generally go online very early in the search. As a result, Internet buyers are not ready to set an appointment and not ready to buy. They are in the research phase.

Why do so few marketers help their sales teams to keep Internet buyers engaged and interested? Can a sales team keep up with a buyer over 290 days? No way. Marketers and sales teams for builders and developers must come together to design and develop a communications strategy that re-engages the buyer over time and gives their new community or new home the best chance of being sold.

New home sales is a great analogy to the dating process. Yet many in the new home construction business have lost the concept of what the proper response and the appropriate timing is for engaging people appropriately and taking the time to find out what they want in a new city, new community and new home.

Jumping immediately to price point and bedrooms and baths is about the same as asking if the person you are dating squeezes the toothpaste from the end or the middle. You need to find out a lot more about a buyer, (for example, identifying lifestyle requirements that could be matched to a specific community) and have numerous strategic conversations (online and offline) before you ask them to tie the knot and sign on the dotted line.

$30 Million Down The Toilet

By Alan Daniel

In the early 2000's, after ten years of financing real estate and start-ups, I was in the middle of my first start-up business

venture. I hired Terry Bradshaw to host a short two-minute paid infomercial series called "TB's Pick of

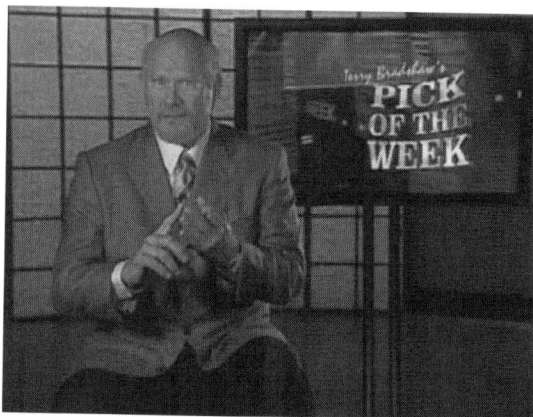

the Week" on MSNBC. Participating companies paid us $30,000 to receive national recognition and a corporate video to use in sales and marketing collaterals. Our sales team called 1,000 prospects per month and closed 1 deal per month. We had a great run, and at the top of the market, we were calling 25,000 to 30,000 prospects and closing 30 deals per month. But eventually the bottom fell out. We went from closing 30 deals a month to 6 deals a month, literally within the same year. Essentially we reached market saturation. We quite literally, ran out of new prospects.

To make matters worse, we weren't effectively collecting data on the prospects. We didn't listen to the prospects which is necessary to survive in business. We were having nearly 3,500 conversations with CEO's each month, yet we didn't track any of the intelligence that would have helped us to understand our market and grow our business.

In real estate, if your sales teams are making any calls at all, it is vital that you listen to your consumer and gather intelligence. Builders and developers would be well-served to know the WHY's behind a buyer's decision to purchase elsewhere and DOCUMENT THEM. I have learned the misses are just as important as the successes. Stepping into the shoes of your buyer will help you determine how to communicate with future buyers and ultimately help them make better decisions. Capturing this critical information improves your planning, product development, floor plan design and location selections.

Letting your sales team be foot loose and fancy-free and failing to document lost opportunities is a bad plan. It obviously does a disservice to your company's future sales. Gold medalists Carl Lewis and Usain Bolt did not get to be the fastest sprinters in the world without a coach to measure their results and push them to do more and change and improve techniques.

Understanding how many calls are being made, how many call-backs sales teams receive, how many calls convert to tours and how many tours convert to sales is absolutely necessary. There is not a sales person out there who shouldn't know their rate of converting calls to tours and tours to contracts.

So what the hell is your sales team doing? If they're not closing contracts and negotiating with real buyers, they need to be calling prospects and documenting activity and conversations so your company can improve. Sales, marketing, land acquisition, product types, price points, floor plans, and more can be improved if you listen to the market.

Don't make the same mistake I made with my Terry Bradshaw's Pick of the Week venture. Use data to help your team evolve and thrive. If we had evolved, we could have probably produced another 1,000+ infomercials, rather than flushing our $30,000,000 business down the toilet.

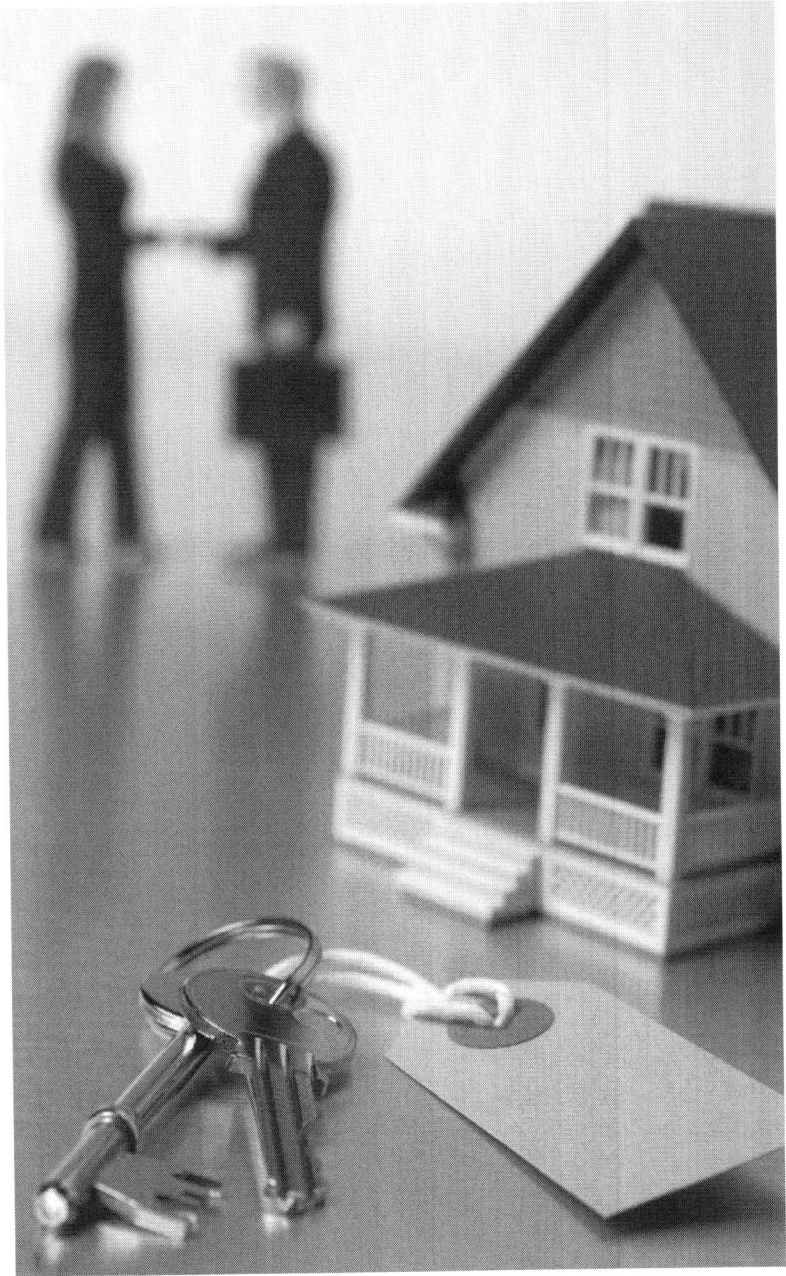

The Key is to Start with the <u>Invitation</u>

By Robert Cowes

Those who focus on the initial connection with the buyer will be most successful in selling new homes, and those who make it easy for buyers to engage early will get more than their two minutes of fame. Television has its place in an advertising campaign, but it is not typically a primary lead generation tool and it is always harder to track your return on investment. There are other channels that provide a more tangible return than TV, primarily because television isn't interactive. There is no engagement - no connection. Not only are TV and traditional media very difficult to track, TV doesn't offer an easy next step for consumers. In the online arena, buyers can engage. They can view a community, neighborhood, or product and immediately request information or schedule a tour. Allowing a consumer to take

the first step in the relationship also allows builders and

developers to track which invitations and Calls to Action

("CTA's") are working. Dollar for dollar, digital marketing

channels are going to yield higher returns and better results

than traditional efforts.

Builders and developers need to measure what engages

home buyers.   According to master-planned community

marketing strategist, Melissa Miller, "Too many times at the

beginning of a project, we recognize that marketers and sales

teams are not aligned, not working together strategically and

not ready to communicate to the prospect at the same time."

A fragmented and isolated approach to online marketing is common with local builders who don't have an integrated system. "This is the builder who is always excited to see the efficiency that can be captured through the use of online tactics to engage buyers," said Miller. To gather intelligence,

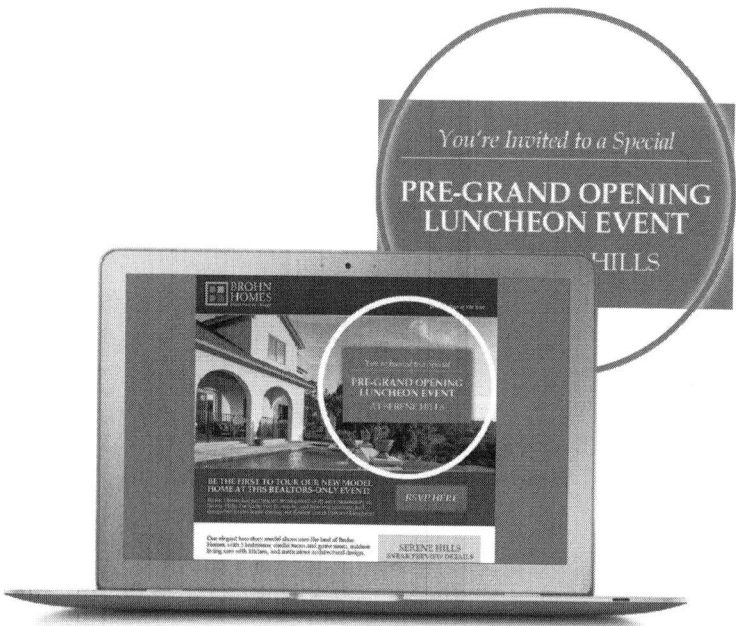

you have to give buyers an opportunity and good reason to connect with you and your products. Arguably one of the most important elements of an effective marketing strategy are effective "Calls to Action". The "invitation" is an active ingredient in the relationship building campaign.

To pin down the perfect "Call To Action' and drive traffic for lead generation, a builder must step back and take a look at whether the information you are providing is valuable to your buyer. We find that home buyers will provide you with valuable information like their e-mail address if you provide floor plans, price sheets, and rare community insights.

Anything you can offer to make meaningful and personal contact with your prospects will increase the effectiveness of your marketing campaigns. Using digital technology, you can make every message unique to your audience with a strong personal offer as simple as community events, news, or data you have collected unique to their interests, such as recent home values in communities where you build. The crazy point here is that technology allows you to know, not guess, exactly what the consumer wants and exactly what "Calls to Action" are driving the most leads and qualified buyers. If you have the right frame of mind, and the tools to help, you can really get to know your prospective buyers. Again, digital advertising allows advertisers and home sellers to leverage new technology, which is not as available with traditional methods such as TV and print. Solid CTA's coupled with technology such as "web tracking" enable your brand to build better relationships with buyers.

It Takes Marketing **AND** Sales

to Build a Relationship

By Alan Daniel

Once you have initiated the relationship with a response to a Call To Action or Invitation, technology allows your marketing campaigns to be an extension of the conversations your sales teams are having offline. Specifically, marketers and sales teams need to work together on the integrated goal of continuous engagement. We encourage developers and builders to stop using antiquated, isolated systems. We often discuss that a paper registration card or a tour visit log is not going to capture the available information marketing needs to follow up intentionally with a buyer. The days of sales teams using Big Chief tablets are gone. Paper systems do not allow marketing and sales teams to "slice and dice" collective data that provides valuable insight for both marketing and sales.

"If a builder uses integrated strategies and technology that supports both marketing and sales teams, a builder will not lose one single lead, and those leads should convert to in-person tours," says Chuck Dennis, a 20-year veteran New Home Specialist. "For example," Chuck continues, "my sales teams are well trained on the communication needs of our home buyers and we have mapped out ALL communication points along the sales cycle."

By preparing and measuring all touch points such as e-mail and offline communications, Chuck and his sales team understand the best time to call a prospect and which subject lines get the highest open and engagement rates. Combining sales calls with timely marketing messages such as neighborhood announcements, recent sales stats, new home buying tips, and personal thank you notes after a web visit, is all part of the integrated multi-touch point system it takes to win the sale. Vince Lombardi said football is a game of inches. New home sales is no different. It is a series of small, accurate, intentional steps from both sales and marketing that advance a relationship and ultimately create the sale.

Now Listen In

By Robert Cowes

Some builders and developers have the following mindset: "I spend all this money on marketing and sales, so where are my contracts?" That's like Jerry Jones saying, "I am a football team owner, I built a grand stadium, I have a big roster of talented athletes. Where is my Super Bowl title?" Now I am not a professional football coach, but I will continue the analogy. Even I know that football teams can't win Super Bowls if they are not measuring the stats: completed passes, first downs, interceptions, successes in the red zone. All the metrics a coach measures are designed to build a Super Bowl winning team.

Builders and developers who are not measuring Calls to Action, Invitations, and Offers are losing the marketing game. Leads generated with various marketing tactics and various invitations are relevant. Tracking "lead source" should be automatic. Tracking Call to Action performance should be a best practice. Understanding "open rates" on e-mail campaigns is important. Further, in order to convert a lead into phone calls, meaningful conversations, tours and ultimately into a contract, you must get out your ruler and start measuring. Measure what is important to your buyers and what engages them at all stages of the relationship. The more you know about your invitations, offers, calls to action, and monthly newsletters, the better you will understand your buyers and the more new homes you will sell.

As an example of what is easily possible with engagement technology, let's look at the grocery business. Grocery stores are now printing coupons based on the items on your receipt. How smart is that?! And dry cleaners offer personalized incentives to buyers who are off their regular schedule. They can track who is "cheating" on them and offer discounts to win back loyal customers. How cool is that?! Builders and developers can use similar technology. At a minimum, a new home builder or developer should track the online habits of their prospects. As mentioned, marketers and sales teams should know which call to action is working and what lead source is consistent.

But more importantly, technology can get more granular. Marketers AND sales teams can see how many times a visitor has been to your website, how many properties have been viewed, and how many e-mail campaigns have been clicked (collectively a "lead score"). Are you looking at this level of detail? You can and you should. It's easy. When you start thinking this way, you'll find your most effective calls to action, offers, and incentives. Then you'll give up on TV and radio, which may be good for feeding the ego, but not necessarily great at filling the pipeline!

Can't See the Forest Through the Trees?

By Robert Cowes

As the old adage goes: a forest is full of beautiful trees for the beholding. But when one becomes so engrossed in looking at the individual trees, he may forget that each tree is merely one of thousands in the forest and thus lose sight of the big picture.

Builders and developers spend billions on infrastructure, equipment, design, and building their vision. In many cases software and sales systems for prospect management are independent of the builder and not on management's radar. It is here that the builder and their sales team often find themselves searching for true north on the compass.

Various statistics support the fact that success depends on such systems. During the downturn of 2007 – 2008, we spoke to the CEO of a technology platform who commented that 75 percent of all builders and developers who failed, or went out of business, did NOT have a CRM for lead management. Of course, that's not the only reason a development or project failed, but it is a high correlation. In contrast, 89 percent of builders and developers who had a CRM survived the downturn.

Another interesting point is that while an organization may have a CRM, 60 percent are not used or what the industry calls adopted. That is a crazy statistic, when it is such an important factor for success.

Why do CRM's fail? One reason: implementation of the technology was a failure. No one adopted it because of terrible set-up and training. Software and technology helps builders and developers keep marketing and sales staff accountable. Implementation includes teaching the sales staff how to use it and what to do after the software is built or purchased. By using a CRM system the sales team knows exactly who needs to be called each day.

A comparison of two projects will put this into perspective for you. In 2006, Project One didn't record a single transaction: zero sales in a year. Project Two, a sister community only a few miles away, did $450M in transactions during 2006. The difference? The builder in Project Two implemented an integrated marketing solution through the use of a CRM, and in less than 12 months generated 1,100 leads and 23 transactions. The only thing that changed was the team and the tactics.

Online marketers often hear, "the leads are no good." According to Chuck Dennis, a 20 year professional Real Estate Sales Consultant, "You don't need more leads, you need to work the leads you have… better. You need a strategy to better farm and better cultivate leads. The answer is not more leads. If you hear your sales team say they don't have good leads that is absolutely a misconception. They don't have a strategy to work the leads."

For a project in Mexico, the sales teams told the developer/builder the leads were bad and they couldn't successfully sell the project. With an integrated marketing and sales technology solution/ CRM which tracked e-mail open rates, and nurtured buyers who clicked on various links, the sales team was able to start conversations. There were so many new conversations that the builder was soon able to fly down 10 prospects every few weeks. Using the same leads that were "no good," but a different strategy, increased leads, increased tours, increased the average price per home and sold more lots.

According to Robert Cowes, "We implemented CRM so all leads from the website and landing pages ran through it". On the sales side, Chuck Dennis implemented a process that leveraged technology to follow up on the leads knowing how and when to touch them. The team rebranded the community and elevated the value proposition along with improving the marketing and sales communications. The call to action to "buy now" call to action, before price increases, created urgency. As a result, sales velocity and absorption increased.

By investing in the brand and implementing a follow up process which leverages technology, the builder was able to turn the project around and turn what the sales team thought were "bad leads" into contracts.

Finding Honey Holes

By Robert Cowes

I love fishing. More than fishing, I love finding the perfect fishing hole: the secret one that only a few friends know about!

In every area of the county, you fish for different catch. So you have your favorite spots and each spot has its own story of success. Interactive marketing is the same. For example, SEM/SEO, non- listing sites/advertising, third party marketing and traditional direct mail are a little like those hard-to-find but gratifying fishing holes. Each is going to yield its own catch.

If you want to fish in the ocean, the best leads will come from your own website. But getting those best leads to your individual site is not easy and takes a good deal of bait. You have to drive traffic (visitors) to the website by using SEM/SEO on home buying and affinity websites related to your product. In addition, that one strategy is not going to be enough to sell all your available inventory. To meet your sales goals, you need to keep fishing.

Next, using listing sites and third party marketing is going to be very effective. Obtaining and renting lists that give you quality leads will be essential. Let's take for example, a "false start on a project". One residential component of an unlaunched master planned community is a perfect case study to drive this example home.

As a result of the 2008 market crash, the community stalled. However, an initial announcement done in 2003 gathered over 5,000 leads in the project's first two years. But because the project never fully launched, the leads were seen as unusable. An integrated campaign with SmartTouch® took 1,500 (30 percent of the five year old leads) leads re-warmed them, and aligned the right prospects with the right builders and developers. Unless you are planning on going out of business, lead generation information is extremely relevant at all stages of a residential project.

There are a lot of factors that go into homebuilding beyond construction. There are also a lot of considerations people make besides price and the number of bedrooms.

These email strategies we deploy are meant to be an engaging and value-adding service. When you are trying to build your database, or when an Internet lead goes dark, you need a systematic approach to re-engage the prospect. If you are using technology, you can track what real estate buyers are reading and collect intelligence on their preference.

If you go back 10 years, builders and developers put up a sign and ran an ad in the real estate section of the local paper. Websites were just getting more refined and were little more than online brochures. Social media, real estate portals, and mass e-mailing platforms didn't exist at all.

Technology now allows us to send an email to 100,000 prospects and to track interested buyers with digital marketing. That means we can cast a wide net AND see what particular lure is of interest. Just like most good fisherman who won't go fishing without the inside scoop on a honey hole, or a great fish finder, you shouldn't start a new home project without knowing your honey hole, a very attractive lure, and a strong plan for building buyers interest.

Keep in mind, different channels will allow you to troll and catch different buyers i.e. different fish. The best leads are website leads that come to your site through search engine marketing or search engine optimization. Next best are leads that come from listing sites, followed by third party email opt in lists and finally, traditional methods.

You can bet a good fisherman knows his tackle box and know which bait, lure and spot to fish in order to get the best and most fish. In real estate marketing, your bait –the content of text, display ads, specialized landing pages rather than general websites, and mobile invitations will drive the right traffic. Your lure is price, amenities or features, depending on your "fish."

It is absolutely critical to understand this analogy. This is not a one bait catches all strategy. A cane pole and a piece of cheese is not going to catch the big fish and casting a wide net will only get you more bait fish. I have gone on too far with this analogy, in order to make a point.

Man, I sure love to fish.

$5 Mil on the Table

By Robert Cowes

Several years ago, a new builder/developer in Texas was deploying a "Whisper" campaign. Essentially, we worked for several months to build interest and leads for an event that would allow buyers to be the first to select their lot for a new development. The campaign yielded 500 specific lead responses to invitations for the one day only event. In addition, we used other channels to ensure success. One week prior to the event a direct mail slick went to each invitee. We made sure more-than-adequate website advertising was placed for timely release. We warmed realtors and sent special invitations, and we were in all the local print publications. Everyone in town who was interested in this kind of event knew it was happening and the leads were warmed and ready to attend.

Unfortunately, the developer didn't use the tools at his disposal. There was no process for registration or making appointments, despite its availability within the SmartTouch software.   We have an appointment and registration module that is easily deployable, but it wasn't used and the results were catastrophic.

On the beautiful morning of the event, only a handful of sales staff, myself and my son were on hand with over 300 people who had come to select their new lot, as promised. The understaffing tragedy was compounded by the lack of a registration process (which also was available in our software via IPad and swipe key). The builder was inundated with 300 interested leads who didn't know who to talk to and where to get key information. The day ended with only 20 registrations.

We needed to convert 1.5% of the 300 attendees to meet our sales goals. We needed 28 total sales. We had 8. It took 3 more months to convert another 20 leads into buyers - and it was all preventable. If there were enough staff in place to handle the expected flow, a system in place to register interested buyers, and had we known exactly what we needed to convert, we could have easily sold 28 units the first day.

I am not a high stakes Las Vegas gambler, I don't know what $5,000,000 looks like on the table, but thanks to that day I do know what $5M left on the table looks like. Frustrating.

The Mis-Step

By Alan Daniel

Why is it that some home builder executives know exactly what needs to be completed to finish a spec home on time and on budget, but have loose ends in sales and marketing? Here's what I mean. SmartTouch® was recently brought in to re-engage a database of 9,000 people. So we did what we do best. We created a compelling email and sent it.

Within 30 minutes, more than 200 recipients said "Contact me now", yet the builder did not notify the sales team. Not even one sales person was available to respond to these200 urgent buyer requests within the same day. Sales and marketing were not aligned. That's like going to the grocery store to pick up a few things, but not having a shopping cart. Have you ever found yourself starting out with just a small basket, then realizing you needed the entire cart? Why not plan ahead and grab the bigger cart? We do it all the time. We don't connect all the dots within the plan we are making. It is absurd.

Terry Bradshaw, in his book, "It's Only a Game" recalls a story about buying a herd of cattle that were to be delivered to his ranch in Oklahoma and not having ranch hands or help to unload the cattle. Alone when the truck arrived, he and the driver made an attempt to unload 100 head of cows down a narrow chute without adequate help. He said, "They were jumping everywhere, it was total chaos, and I knew better. That is the last time I will fall for that trick." Just as Terry will be prepared for his next load of cattle, I assure you our client who sends an email to 9,000 people will have more than one person available to field calls from hundreds of buyers all wanting to talk at the same time.

Another misstep that we have seen is builders and developers spending $30,000 on a well-designed and branded website and not spending money on traffic attraction (monthly Adword and SEO budgeting). That is like creating a gorgeous print ad and never running it in a magazine or newspaper. And it happens every day.

One more example of our industry's lost opportunities is the common neglect of international markets. Toronto, Canada is as big a market for Florida retirement homes as the northeast pockets of the U.S. yet developers consistently ignore these international buyers. To me, that's as neglectful as a car dealership shutting its doors on Labor Day weekend. Ridiculous.

The simple yet obvious lesson is to ensure your strategies for sales and marketing are well aligned and integrated so you can capture new traffic

and quickly move them from "online to pipeline"

collectively. In fact, we believe this so strongly, "online to pipeline" is one of our corporate mottos, and we use it daily.

A Bird of a Different Feather

By Alan Daniel

Speaking of ignoring international markets, selling real estate in Canada is different than selling real estate in the U.S. Looking at the differences and similarities can be of use to new home builders and developers in both markets. Nick Eveleigh of PMA Brethour and I met at the 2010 International Builder's Show in Florida. Within the first half hour, we found opportunities to improve the real estate sales process in both Canada and the US.

According to Nick, "The real estate trends in Canada have been fairly stable over the last five years, unlike the American market. Though investor markets have taken a bit of a dip, it has simply caused us to work a bit harder to find our buyers." However, marketing and technology are absolutely new to home builders and developers in Canada. Traditionally, builders and developers would put up a sign, gather registrants and begin working the leads to identify buyers. Eveleigh described one recent example of a 420 condo unit building launched to Realtors, who initially sold 230 units. Within three weeks of the launch, they were selling one to two units per week and had no additional leads. Again and again in the Canadian real estate market, a project will put up a sign and generate as many as 3,000 prospective leads. But there could be a delay in follow up with leads and if a project is just being announced there could be four or more months delay for opening. When sales staff start to follow up, they find that because they didn't immediately engage the lead, prospects have bought elsewhere or are no longer interested. They have gone dark.

In Canada, the new "must have" and "must do" for home builders and developers is no different from the US market.

1. Get a sign up on the property early.

2. Get a registration site that will capture registrant data.

3. Create local awareness.

4. Design your website correctly and maximize SEO.

5. Use Google Adwords to generate more effective leads.

The difference between the Canadian real estate market and the US real estate market is that the Canadian market's online search and technology solutions are in their infancy. Nick says, "Technology is going to revolutionize the way we do business in Canada. Our team has the expertise to bring to the table and it's a real game changer to be the first to market. PMA Brethour believes this is a great time to be in this industry, and a great time to adopt new technology to serve online buyers differently than in the past".

Canada is one of the largest markets in North America with some of the coolest architecture in the world. It is interesting to see the market's adoption of technology and how it is used slightly differently than by American developers.

If you're a Canadian reading this book, you should study how revenue-starved builders and developers in the US built buyer leads through a downturn, as you can learn from it. If you're a US builder, you should take note of how Canada will adopt new technologies, as they just may skip a few generations and leap frog the US as they begin to invest online. New home builders and developers can learn from what they are doing north of the U.S. border. I sure have.

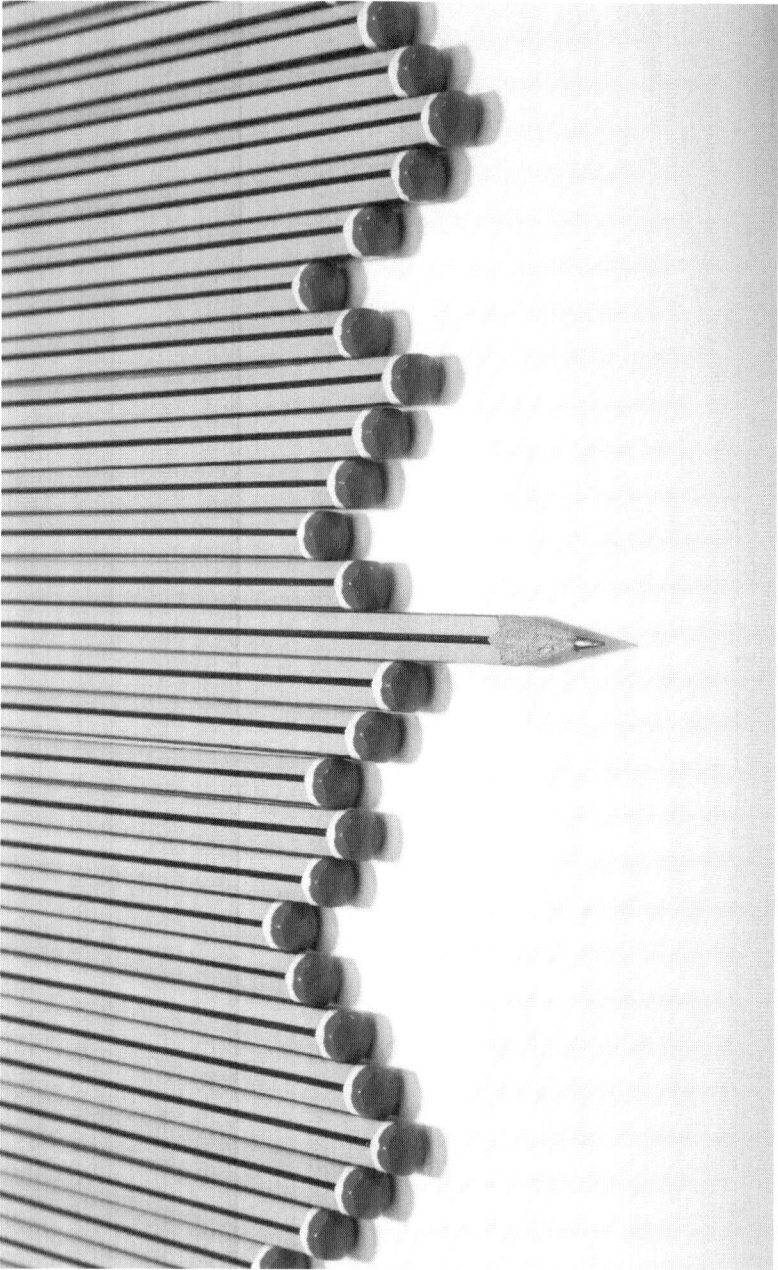

The Same, But Different

By Alan Daniel

"When everybody zigs, zag," says Marty Neumeier author of brand strategy book, *ZAG and THE BRAND GAP*. Neumeier attempts to answer the age-old question of how brands can harness the power of differentiation. The author argues that companies need "radical differentiation" to create lasting value. The unique perspective of this author illustrates how keeping up with the competition is no longer a winning strategy. Today you have to out-position, out-maneuver, and out-design the competition. The new rule?

When everybody zigs, zag.

Take for example a 100 -year-old brand, which, in many cases could become tired, run down and outdated. Yet – from a branding perspective, our industry can stand to learn from the Girl Scouts. You may not have a 100-year-old brand, but you can learn from one. The lesson: be consistent in your messaging and in your brand. Don't be all things to all people. Understand your brand promise and deliver your content and marketing strategies to deliver that promise. Be consistent in action, in your website, in how you interact with people, in your marketing, and in everything you do. But innovate and engage your consumer.

A real estate advertising expert, Dave Miles of Miles DNA, ask builders and developers to consider, "What is your brand promise?" Differentiation is how you deliver a complex message to the consumer. If you don't understand your brand promise, your prospective will arrive at this conclusion at one of two ways. You will tell them how you are different and help them to understand your value, or they will figure it out for themselves and you will never know. David Miles is one of the 50 most influential people in the real estate industry, and he tells the story that 50 percent of people living in a Lennar home could not tell you who the builder was after 5 years in a home. But they knew what car they drove. A $300,000 purchase and no brand memory on one of the biggest purchases a family will make in their lifetime.

We all know Apple. The brand is built around design and around a competitive advantage. But in the home building industry we don't communicate our value as well as a $500 device. As an industry, we have a difficult time communicating our value of new, well designed, construction. Why can't we do cool things with technology like Apple? We can, but we have to be able to start to embrace the importance of it to sell it to buyers. We can portray the lifestyle and the experience in our design and communications.

As the CEO of a digital advertising agency and technology firm of which I'm CEO, typically brings strategy back to digital tactics that can be successfully executed. We discuss brand differentiation as a crucial step in a home builder's and developer's maturation process, but once that is accomplished, we believe quality messaging must be executed well online.

Therefore, we can cannot emphasize enough the importance of how your online presence and brand is reflected on your website. A home buyer begins their search on the internet and can find various brands within seconds. How many opportunities are missed in our online branding efforts because we failed to stay relevant, innovative and engage our prospects? Are we watching, paying attention, and finding ways to connect to buyers? Could we find ways to save perfect strangers from their exhaustive, impersonal home searches by adding value, and giving them what they need to make a decision? If we don't add quality content and value during the search process, why would a buyer believe a builder will provide quality construction and solid warranties?

We live in a world of "make it my way" and "I want it now." As a quality builder, don't miss the opportunity to make your brand zig-zag past the competition.

In New Homes & Websites, You Get What You Pay For!

By Robert Cowes

There's no such thing as a standard website. There are standard templates for websites, much like there are basic floor plans (a kitchen, a living room, a bedroom, a bathroom and a closet.)

Building a website is a lot like building a house. Are you talking basic necessities - four walls and roof? Or a McMansion to be showcased on the next episode of "Cribs"? Two-bedroom, one-bath starter? Or mud rooms and master suites?

Websites are a complex blend of strategy, content, aesthetics and technology. And everyone's needs and desires differ. So if you find yourself struggling to determine what you are paying for in terms of a website, let me challenge you with this thought. Ninety-nine percent of home buyers go to the Internet first before ever setting foot in a model home. How much did you pay to furnish and decorate your most recent model home? What did you pay for your most recent website? Same buyer, different experience. The amount you spend merchandising a model home has a direct correlation to the amount you should consider spending on a website.

Here's why. Your website is a reflection of your model home. It represents the lifestyle and location of the new home buyer. So great photography, floor plan renderings and graphic merchandising are just as important as the inside of the model home itself.

We equate creating a website to communicate your brand to the way we communicate selling homes.

#1 - Let's call it manufactured housing. If you need a basic tool to communicate your services, beliefs or opinions, we can make it easy. There are numerous off-the-shelf templates that we can customize slightly to reflect your brand. You provide the content and images and we can get you up and blogging in no time. You can even change your format and color palette according to your mood.

#2 - A home makeover. So you already have a site with decent curb appeal but maintenance is a hassle and you need a little updating? If you need your existing site overhauled with an open-source CMS, we can send in the crew one last time and from there on you can maintain everything yourself. Unless of course, you need to call us back for heavy lifting branding and messaging.

#3 - A starter home. For that first-time website buyer, we have a few plans to get you up and running in no time.

Choose from one of three custom designs, a site with a nice look and your basic necessities. You don't need to overcomplicate things.

#4 - The move up. Your needs have changed and space is a little cramped. You've done it before and learned what you would do differently next time. This budget range will get you into a new site with custom design, well-written content, numerous options, accessories, and reports - something you finally feel is your own. With proper planning, you should be able to stay here a while, and track where all your friends are coming from.

#5 – The Good Life. Did you say a neighborhood with amenities? Swimming pools? Tennis courts? Playgrounds? You've moved beyond the basics and are looking for some luxuries. Video galleries, interactive maps, virtual tours, conversion reports. And you want a high-traffic area? OK, so maybe not your typical neighborhood request. But there comes a point where having your site is great but you need to see some traffic on the sidewalk. We can help you get the home you are looking for, and we can deliver visitors to your door with some standard search engine optimization.

#6 - Finally, your oceanfront dream home. You want an eco-friendly six-bedroom, hurricane-proof beach house with a home theater. No worries, it's only technology. If you really need a new brand identity, up-to-the-minute-tweets, Flickr, YouTube and Facebook feeds, and other custom features out the ying-yang, let's get started. But first we will need to architect that blue print. Websites over $50,000 begin with a $5,000 discovery that defines the strategy and scope, designs the plan, and delivers the final estimate for your approval. It's a killer house, and you have every right to expect a great return on investment!

It doesn't matter how beautifully staged the inside of the house may be. If the foundation is crumbling and the roof is about to cave in, there is no point in dressing up the inside. Similarly, it doesn't matter how beautiful a website is if it is not built to win the online traffic game. We won't get into SEO tactics in this book, as we can write hundreds of chapters on the complexity of it, but we will talk about some common mistakes that builders and developers make when they decide to build a website. We work with many builders and developers where we inherit an existing website that is not getting the job done. We see the same mistakes often.

Robert Cowes, SmartTouch® Interactive Co-Founder and President, tells clients the following:

1. A big mistake is the lack of keyword research to determine what is being searched for by your specific buyers. You can have a killer website, but if you don't have any

traffic visiting the website, it doesn't do you any good. The key is to drive traffic to the website. That's like having a great model home with luxury furnishings and high end finishes, which no one tours. But you can't drive traffic, and no one can tour the model, if you don't know where the "house" is located. Keyword research is analogous to the address of the home. It has to be published. Again, we aren't going to get into details on SEO because you need an expert to help in this area. You didn't decorate that model home yourself, right?

2. To expand further, when you start to build your website make sure every title, description, tags (if applicable), and keyword is intentional and purposeful, specifically talking about content. You don't need to bold keywords or keep a high density of keywords in the content itself so long as you are writing quality content that is unique (never been talked about before in this exact manner) and on topics that will

attract and engage. If this sounds like Greek, that is because a necessary but specific function follows searching the keywords, developing content, marrying tags to content and ensuring all the pieces match. Typically, you need someone well-versed in SEO to help set up this specificity.

3. Next, cover more ground for leads by writing blog posts and pages about specific neighborhoods, the styles of homes within those neighborhoods, events and activities from your perspective, market reports titled with the detailed month and year you're focusing on, and answers to questions buyers and sellers may have. People tend to research answers to questions rather than general information on a topic. By creating unique content, you are helping Google drive traffic to your well-optimized website. By completing these tasks and setting up your website properly, it will work long after you've left the desk. People will experience the lifestyle and location before and after they have seen the model home. In

addition, your differentiation will increase your probability of selling more projects and converting traffic from a valuable "digital location" into profitability.

4. Forgetting the most critical aspect of your website is a mistake 9.5 out of 10 new customers make every day. Leaving the Call to Action (CTA) off of the primary target area on your website will cause you to lose leads. Unfortunately, it is also one of the easiest fixes, if you know just a few of the tricks.

Interested VS Invested?

By Alan Daniel

New products are launching left and right. ; Apps are making life easier every instant. Here's the problem: being interested in this stuff is fun, but how are you going to use it to add value in your business?

Borrell and Associates, an Internet marketing firm that tracks online trending reported recently, "Eighty-seven percent of real estate buyers look online, but the majority of builders and developers only have 41 percent of their marketing budget online." Revealing the fact that more developers are "interested" than "invested".

According to Cisco, by the year 2015 annual Internet traffic will reach a zettabyte; almost 200 times the total size of all words ever spoken by humans. Furthermore, the number of connected devices around the globe is predicted to rise to 50 billion+ within five years. So what does all of this technology jargon mean to the hopeful, driven, home builder? It means accessing information about your community, your available home sites, and your custom home for sale is going to become even easier for consumers.

Being interested in lead generation, discussing it as an option for a marketing strategy and thinking about how you might use this tool is already outdated. Atari video games and Sony Walkmans are still being sold (somewhere), but does that make them relevant today? Do you really want to hire a retro advertising agency, which was a powerhouse in the 80's and is still talking about the Internet in terms of "hits"? No.

In order to sell $100,000,000 annually in new homes, not only do you need capital, knowledge of land acquisition, and a proven operational process, you need to be invested in technology and tactics that will drive not 100 people ("unique visitors") to your website, but 10,000 possible buyers to your website. Our interactive technology company is fortunate do just that for many builders and developers at the top of their markets. We get to see what it takes to grow. We are a part of the team that has helped take a builder from 10 homes per year to 800. We are not the only reason our clients succeed, but we are a big part of why they sleep well at night and can confidently talk to their investors, partners, employees, and spouse about their ability to sell 20, 50, or even 100 homes per month. These aggressive builders and developers are not slightly interested in online; they are fully invested. Are you?

To sell $100,000,000 in real estate requires commitment to a lot of things. From our technology perspective, it requires a digital investment, not merely an interest online. If you are interested, read on and do nothing. If you are invested, pick up the phone and pull the trigger on those online decisions you've been holding back on.

How to Stretch Your Marketing Dollar

By Robert Cowes

Your team of trades/subs are great and produce quality results, plus they are reliable, if they weren't, you wouldn't use them. Why would you look at your marketing sub any differently? Would buyers want to finish out their covered patio, or their upgrade all their finishes? Perhaps for the fixer-upper, flipper or cost-conscious buyer, but not for a first home buyer, and certainly not a luxury home buyer. You aren't going to rely on something as important as your brand and your buyer to a vender who only works on marketing at night or a as side job, are you? You will be much more satisfied if you hire a professional. Is your marketing team a trade partner or DIYer?

If you're not convinced and don't want to go all in, you can adopt a "crawl, walk, run" strategy. Start slow. For builders and developers just starting, here is what my team recommends: "Crawl" first on a small budget:

Purchase and implement a CRM and integrate it into sales and marketing strategies.

❖ Develop Realtor outbound blasts and lead nurturing campaigns to your own prospects.

❖ Drive some traffic to your site with ads on Google (small budget).

❖ Syndicate your listings on home buying websites.

These strategies will allow your sales team and marketing efforts to track conversations, develop reminders and nurture leads. Owning your leads and tracking buyers in a CRM database you control is an essential part of developing an independent sales strategies and is a great start. If you rely on the Realtor community exclusively, you are allowing that broker to own that prospect. If they follow up, it is on their timeline, not yours. If they fail to set a reminder about a prospect who is interested in a year out project purchase, you lose that lead. If the broker has other properties, interests or life events, you miss the opportunity to reach the consumer directly.

You need to stay top of mind with local Realtors, so send your new sales person to Realtor offices to be a part of their weekly meetings. Realtors are a source of qualified leads, so treat them as a customer and educate them on how you build and offer value in your homes. We aren't suggesting that small builders and developers cut ties with the Realtor community, we just don't recommend putting all the marketing eggs in one basket.

"Walk" by implementing all the above, then adding some of these to the mix:

- ❖ Custom content creation
- ❖ Specific landing pages
- ❖ Email to 3rd party lists and new databases

❖ Digital display advertising on home builder sites and affinity portals

Now it is time to hire a part-time writer to write fresh content. Press releases, new pages, white pages or links - a freelance writer will charge by the project for a fast and economical solution to content. The writer needs to know your community and needs to be able to provide valuable conversations to the public to order to increase traffic. Most builders and developers wouldn't trust your average freelance writer to hang drywall, for the same reason we suggest hiring professional writers to write website content. Builders and developers should also have their writers create content for blogs, Facebook, LinkedIn, email blasts, and other outlets. People will come back to your site if you are delivering information that is engaging and relevant to their specific interests.

Adding search ability and analytical tracking will give you hard data on what is working online and what isn't. You must give yourself and your team the ability to be flexible with your marketing dollars during the year. If something isn't working, change it. If leads are coming from one source, allocate more to those resources. Analytics take the guesswork out of advertising. Your participation in portals like Trulia or New Home Source allows you to test where buyers are coming from. Only technology will track the original lead source. With no margin for error, you can use technology to exactly track the source of your best leads and the source that is converting leads to buyers.

Now that you've dipped your toe in the pool, increase your budget in the places that are referring to you. It's time to buy premium advertising in those locations, add more search opportunities and really make your website start working for you. Whatever is working, do more of it. "Run" by implementing all above and simply adding:

❖ MEASURE! MEASURE! MEASURE!
❖ License a professional to manage your interactive

- ❖ Bump up your purchase of Google advertising by community

- ❖ Buy Premium Ads on portal sites and preferred listings (so yours appear first)

- ❖ Revamp your website

Get a facelift! It is rare for real estate developers to have interactive, stimulating and engaging websites. This is a perfect opportunity for differentiation. Allow a design firm to add photographs, slideshows, interactive floor plans and form captures that will feed your CRM database. It is time to get traffic to the website. What drives transactions at great new home communities? TRAFFIC. The same is true for the Internet. Google Analytics will give you the traffic count of Adwords and will help you establish how to drive traffic.

But more than that, you need to get creative. Embrace the technology that is available for your website. David Miles of Miles DNA Branding recently spoke at the International Builder's Show and said, "With the value of using video today, we as builders and developers should do something cool. Last year, 456.6 million content videos were watched and 105.4 billion video ads were viewed. Viewers spent 2.5 times more time watching personally relevant short form videos compared with other videos." The cost of video production has decreased drastically. For about $500, you can shoot some amazing thirty-second footage highlighting amenities, the building process, land, scenery and local happenings and events.

Kick The Door In

By Robert Cowes & Alan Daniel

The first thing you learn in real estate sales is that traffic counts. But the second thing you should learn is that counting the traffic counts MORE! Remember, it's all about benchmarks and measuring datasets. As a builder, you wouldn't build off the beaten path without a reason and strategy. So knowing that everyone who buys a custom home will go to your website, and the most likely lead conversions are specifically related to the traffic on your website, how can you question a website overhaul? At the very least, a portion of your marketing budget should be dedicated to website improvements? Not just functional, but a traffic heavy site. Traffic is traffic. And traffic converts to leads and leads convert to tours....so on and so forth.

For those who want to dominate their market, create a monthly budget with strategies to include everything we have discussed and the final touches of:

a. Advanced SEO tactics with an outside firm leading the strategy.

b. Public Relations above and beyond custom content creation.

c. Increased budgets in what is working, or more of everything.

d. **MEASURE! MEASURE! MEASURE! EVERYTHING!**

After years of pared-down marketing efforts and a reliance on the Realtor/broker community—during which time social media exploded into a major player on the marketing scene and shoppers increasingly took searches online—many builders and developers are facing a brave new world of new home sales strategies. Those who have utilized a crawl, walk, run method know the benefits of dipping their toe in the pool. You should too. Your benefit is picking up this short read. Start by kicking the door in, when everyone else is still learning to walk or run, or better yet, still using the old strategies. "Kicking the door in" is budgeting half a percent to two percent of gross sales to the marketing budget, using a measured approach to optimizing the campaign, and then beating the competition!

Imagine a World

By Alan Daniel

In today's digital world, if you're not aggressively using technology to market yourself and make your sales process more efficient, you're not going to survive. It's that simple. The world around you is changing, and you need team members around you who study these changes and who know the next moves being made online.   Just as you study that land contract and new advancements in green building techniques, we geeks are studying the next move Google is going to make that will drive more traffic to our builder's websites. Did you hear of Panda, the move to remove "exact match" domain results on Google that crippled millions of online businesses? Of course you didn't. Why would you?

You were putting out a fire or making your next big bet. When the geeks get together, we talk about the latest and greatest technology. We imagine a world where Pandora-type real estate search portals will allow a user to type in their previous three addresses. Then, similar to product recommendation software, our real estate portals will recommend the perfect neighborhood and home for you based on a match of hundreds of variables extracted from your last three homes/neighborhoods.

My staff and I attend many technology conferences annually to study what other industries are up to: new technologies that wow the market. Did you know that 3D printing is not about seeing through a photo in three dimensions, but rather a printer that can build tiny 3D models instantly, easily, cheaply? How are builders and developers going to use that? Imagine being able to enter a CAD drawing for your new design and floor plan, and being able to hand a prospect their new home in a 5 X 8 plastic model that they can take home and show their family and neighbors. How awesome is that?!

Imagine a world, very close to Minority Report, where Tom Cruise is walking next to personal glass billboards with custom messages exactly targeted to his interests. These technologies exist today. We see this with retargeting where our builders and developers' ads follow interested prospects on every future website after they've visited the builder's site. Couple this technology with the technology Corning Glass has developed that allows any and every piece of glass to become a touch screen computer, and voila, we have the same experience as Tom Cruise's character did through only the power of animation and cinema magic.

Take it a step further in top metropolitan markets. Imagine a new home buyer in downtown Toronto, Chicago, New York, Houston or Austin being able to view available floor plans and units in a high rise on a Sunday morning at 2 A.M. by simply walking up to a closed sales center and viewing a glass wall 10-feet tall with an animated rendering of a future phase and Tower III of the high rise. With one swipe of a finger, not even touching the glass, a new couple heading in from a long night out can quickly view available units and price ranges without even needing to talk to sales person or come back during office hours. Tomorrow? No, that is today! I personally know the developers working on such great technology. I have seen it. It works.

Imagine a world in which your buyers are searching for their homes using social media where they can immediately see which friends of friends live in your community. This is not far off, as LinkedIn has already mastered "connections" methodology. A company called Back Porch was purchased by Home Away, and it provides that exact technology and service to online buyers and searchers.

Imagine your consumers searching for a new home and seeing peer reviews from strangers; similar to Yelp for home shopping. Rather than peer reviews for small businesses, we will soon be seeing peer reviews for new home communities, and possibly even a single resale home for sale. Imagine a consumer knowing everything about a resale home all the way down the stain in the carpet or burn mark on the custom wood floor from an iron falling on it, to reviewing a shared social real estate portal, rather than having to visit the property.

Imagine a world where a consumer and custom builder meet on an online matching service like the hundreds of niche dating websites. Why not?

Imagine a world in which a mobile phone will be better than a Realtor because it recommends new home tours based on a geographic targeted auto-alert using exact locations. I can just see it now.

I am a new home buyer. I'm running from one business meeting to another, but my phone notices an hour break in an area where I had previously searched a new home community. I get a text saying, do you have a minute to tour a new phase of the community? Rather than spending my Saturday touring the neighborhood, I knock it out between meetings. How happy will my family be when I tell them my phone found our next new home on a Tuesday at 2 P.M. during a work break?

None of these examples are far-fetched at all. Most of these ideas are already in existence or in motion. On top of these innovations, we are seeing changes every day, and while our industry is not the fastest adopter of new technologies, our consumers are.

If we want to keep up, we have to pay attention to technology and how new home buyers expect to use it to make finding a new home easy. No one wants to expend energy on tasks that technology can simplify for them. There's an app for everything, and apps for marketing and selling new homes deserve your attention. They are already out there. Are you using them to their fullest potential? I promise you, builders and developers who hope to sell

$100,000,000 in new homes are. Whether you're trying to sell 4 or 400 new homes a month, you need to invest in new online marketing and sales technology. It's out there. It's affordable, and it's working.

About Alan Daniel

An accomplished entrepreneur and sales and marketing specialist, Alan Daniel has a proven track record of creating innovative marketing solutions for the real estate industry. He is co-founder and CEO of SmartTouch® Interactive, one of the top lead generation and marketing services companies in North & Latin America. In his role, he oversees business development, strategic partnerships, investor relations and finance. Prior to co-founding SmartTouch® Interactive and the company's flagship product, SmartTouch® CRM, a lead management and email marketing CRM platform for real estate, he helped LandsofAmerica.com triple its business. Working with low-density developers, advertising agencies and rural Realtors, Alan drove lead generation using online advertising and search engine marketing tactics. He also developed interactive marketing solutions for high-end luxury condo developers in Chicago including MetroSceneTV.com, a television program showcasing the city's hottest properties.

About Robert Cowes

As co-founder and president of Austin, Texas-based SmartTouch® Interactive, Robert is an accomplished entrepreneur with expertise in product management, design and execution of lead generation programs, branding, real estate marketing, CRM product management, interactive marketing, and account service.

Robert has managed more than $25 million in demand generation budgets in the last eight years as key executive of SmartTouch Interactive and multiple interactive firms and agencies, yielding 400,000 leads and that have led to $500 million in sales. Robert earned a bachelor's in business administration with a double major in finance and marketing from St. Edward's University in Austin, and a master's in business administration with a specialization in international business from Texas State University in San Marcos. He has been a member of the American Marketing Association since 2005 and actively serves in leadership. Originally from Panama City, Panama, Robert is a former college and semi-pro baseball player.

SMARTTOUCH
I N T E R A C T I V E

SmartTouch® Interactive is an interactive marketing agency that provides proven lead generation programs and a lead management system, SmartTouch® Platform. The SmartTouch® team's expertise in lead generation and online marketing helps firms that require a multi-touch sales cycle that creates demand for products and services and grow their business with customized, interactive lead generation programs and a lead cultivation. Backed by 30 years of experience in developing lead generation programs for hundreds of clients, SmartTouch® sets a new standard with lead generation programs and a single solution that integrates CRM, Marketing Automation, EMail Marketing and Inventory Management in one platform, SmartTouch®.
http://www.smarttouchinteractive.com

Smart Touch List of First and Only:

#1: We opened the floodgates of leads.

SmartTouch is the first to build a lead hub. We were the first to pull leads from all the property portals directly into your SmartTouch account. Buyers can come into your prospect database from hundreds of places. Why not have them flow easily and immediately into your SmartTouch account?

We have opened the floodgates for builders and developers. No more damming up the lead flow. No more running uphill and importing leads from spreadsheets.

We were first to spot the problem and the first to fix it. SmartTouch keeps leads flowing freely.

Note for above: We should Show logos from all the portals. Leverage new home feed list. If we send these independently, we can use CTA such as, "Schedule a call to learn more about lead collection in our smart lead hub."

#2: Database Gardening

SmartTouch was the first to systematically update your prospects' email status and weed out bad email addresses to keep your database CLEAN & protect your email sender reputation. We keep your data cleaner than anyone and we were the first and only lead management platform to clean your data using our smart technology.

#3: We have unleashed the Realtor database.

We are the first and only to offer UNLIMITED Realtor blasts and a DO IT YOURSELF option. Stop paying per-send fees. We have freed the Realtor list. It wanted to be unlocked so we released it. Thanks for helping us be the first to free your local Realtor database.

Note: I realize we need to announce this independently and promote as a product, but this could be a teaser campaign.

#4: We let you show the love to Relocation leads.

SmartTouch was the first to partner with relocation guide magazines and websites to get more leads to SmartTouch builders and developers. Relocation guide buyers need love too. They need more than a distant cousin to educate them on a new town. Who better to educate relocation buyers than SmartTouch builder clients? We help you connect with buyers moving into your city before they even get to town. We are the first and only company to auto-populate and auto-respond to new relocation buyers helping you make the FIRST Impression. Literally!!!!

#5: We put the RIP to the RSVP.

SmartTouch is the first in the US to offer an event manager for builders and developers, eliminating the stress of manual appointment booking. Learning from our Canadian champions, we were the first to offer builders and developers in the US an app to run and manage events smoothly.

#6: Focus Pocus...We are magic!

SmartTouch was the first to turn online registrations into a FREE online focus group. Especially in robust markets and neighborhoods, we noticed people are willing to fill out more items on a registration form. Working with a few brilliant agency partners, we were the first to convert a simple SmartTouch online registration form into a survey. This simple SmartTouch feature allows SmartTouch builder to create free online focus groups. Why pay $10,000+ for a focus group when you can do it for free with SmartTouch?

#7: We invented the first Lead defibrillator.

We were the first to offer custom re-engagement campaigns for the industry that include 1-click preference update links at the top of emails. That makes it easy for buyers to tell you what they want with a click. Like the defibrillator used in ER rooms, our re-engagement feature zaps buyers back to life!

18377125R00079